To my C's – Thank you for the strength to stand tall and for allowing me to grow. Colossians 2:6-7

To my sister tribe – You are the volume to my voice. Thank you for your resounding and never-ending support.

This is a work of fiction. Names, characters, places and incidents either are the product of the author's imagination or are used fictitiously.

Copyright © 2021 Christine T. Leung

All rights reserved. No part of this book may be reproduced or used in any manner without the prior written permission of the copyright owner, except for the use of brief quotations in a book review. For information regardng permission, write to the publisher at email legacpublishing@gmail.com

ISBN: 978-1-7373561-0-3
ISBN: 978-1-7373561-1-0

Library of Congress Control Number: 2021910565
First paper edition: June 2021

Edited by: Millie Godwin & Andrea O'Malley
Content contributor: Cydney Leung
Illustrated by: Su En Tan
Design cover contributor: Amy Kwong

LEGAC
PUBLISHING

What I See

Anti-Asian racism from the eyes of a child

Written by Christine T. Leung
Illustrated by Su En Tan

Note to Parents and Caregivers

What I See is intended for children 8 years and up as an easy-to-follow lyrical picture book on anti-Asian racism from the child's own perspective.

The rise of hate and violence towards Asians and Pacific Islanders in the wake of the pandemic infiltrates our lives and our children's lives.

This book can help you feel more prepared to discuss such a heavy topic with young children. There are sample questions and child-friendly definitions to help guide the conversation.

I hope reading this story will provide some eye-opening reflections, encourage rich dialogue, and empower our youth to get actively involved in countering racism and xenophobia.

A story inspired by every **brave** girl or boy who has been mistreated because of the **color** of their skin or the **shape** of their eyes.

Prologue

You may see me as someone
who always seems fine, a supporting
character who knows her lines.

You may see me as someone
who will never disagree.

This is the story they tell
of who I should be.

But that is all a myth, a fairytale not real.
It's something made up of how I should feel.

When the **coronavirus** came along,
another fictional storyline took shape.

It portrayed Asians and Pacific Islanders
as **villains**, a new target to hate.

So I will **rewrite** this tale
to show you how things should be.

In my own words, from my heart,
a **true** story of **what I see**.

I see you.
I see you through my brown
crescent-shaped eyes.

I see all of the wonderful
parts that make you the
person you are inside.

But because my eyes are shaped differently, some people think I should be treated badly.

But our silence gets us nowhere and only makes things worse. There are signs that make me see that I need to **do more work**.

So I won't ignore what's happening and cannot let it be.
I will use my voice to shout exactly what I see.

In my eyes, hate has no shape or form because I see beyond what you look like or which race you were born.

Even though we are not the same
and may have **different** eyes,
you are still **beautiful**, and so am I.

I see a world so big and so wide. You can fit in just about anywhere, if only you tried.

Yet, some will say that I don't belong here or will ask why I came. But your home is my home, and no one is really to blame.

When we **open** our eyes
to a world beyond our own,

we can begin to make a **difference**
and help change all that's going on.

So, let's fight the virus rather than each other.
That is the only way we can fully recover.

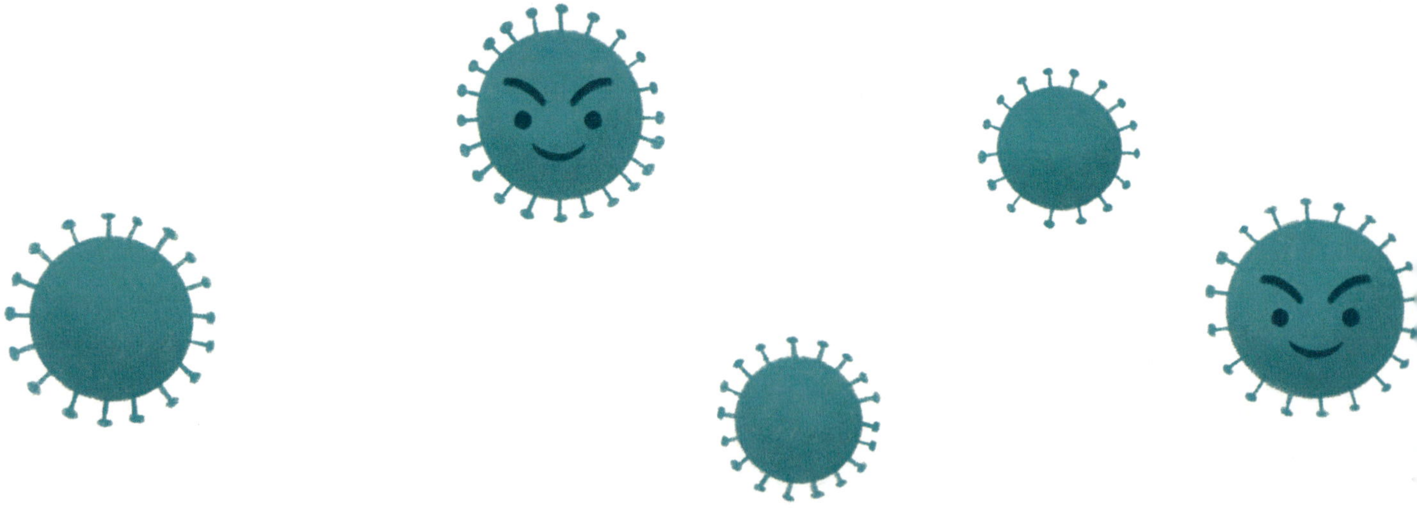

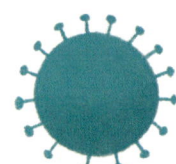
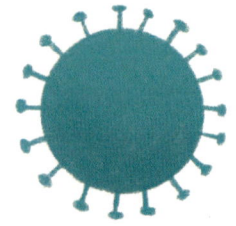

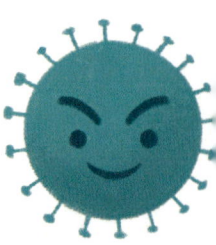

I dream of the day when we can throw away our masks. But until that day comes, I have just **one thing** to ask.

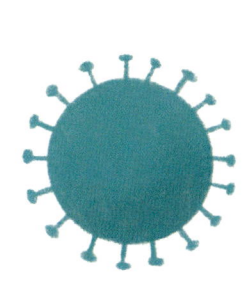   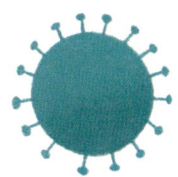 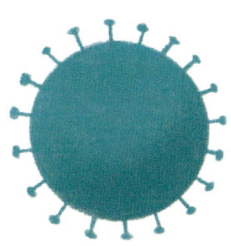

Please hate the virus, **just don't hate me** –

because **I see you**, and now I hope you finally **see me**.

Conversation starters

* Why do you think the girl was treated badly?

* How did that make her feel?

* Has anyone ever called you a name? And how did you feel?

* What motivated the girl to speak up?

* How does she want us to view others who are different?

* Who or what does she think we should be fighting?

* What are things you can do to combat racism or help in your community?

* What do you want others to see in you?

Child-friendly definitions

* **CORONAVIRUS:** A type of virus that has crown-like thorns on the surface

* **CRESCENT:** The shape of a half-moon

* **FICTIONAL:** Made up, not factual

* **PANDEMIC:** Widespread disease that affects a whole country or the entire world

* **RACISM:** Treating people unfairly because of the color of their skin

* **XENOPHOBIA:** Disliking people from countries other than your own

* **VIRUS:** A tiny germ you can't see that can make you sick

Made in the USA
Las Vegas, NV
19 July 2021